All Kinds of
Feelings

Written by Judith Heneghan

Illustrated by Ayesha Rubio

FRANKLIN WATTS
LONDON•SYDNEY

First published in Great Britain in 2019
by The Watts Publishing Group
Copyright © The Watts Publishing Group 2019

Designer: Little Red Ant
Editor: Nicola Edwards

HB ISBN: 978 1 4451 6044 3
PB ISBN: 978 1 4451 6045 0

Printed in Dubai

Franklin Watts
An imprint of Hachette Children's Group
Part of The Watts Publishing Group
Carmelite House
50 Victoria Embankment
London EC4Y 0DZ
An Hachette UK Company

www.hachette.co.uk
www.franklinwatts.co.uk

Contents

Feelings matter.

Things that happen around us affect how we feel inside.

And how we feel inside often shows on the outside.

The way we feel may change
many times throughout the day.

It's my
birthday and
I feel excited!

I feel impatient.
When's the party
going to start?

Now I
feel shy.

6

Grandpa arrives and makes me feel special!

Thank you!

I'm so happy!

I feel sad when we say goodbye.

Or perhaps you feel excited?

Doing something new can make you feel proud!

I feel amazing!

I feel relieved.

I did it! Phew!

I feel very proud.

It can make
other people
feel proud of
you, too!

It's natural to feel curious about the world around us.

Questions bubble up inside, bursting to escape.

What is it like to live under a log?

Why do spiders build webs?

We wonder, we daydream.

And sometimes we feel impatient!

Hurry up, butterfly!

Everyone makes mistakes or has
an accident, now and then.

When we feel embarrassed, our cheeks may grow hot or change colour. It doesn't last very long.

Next time I'll look where I'm going!

Luckily, accidents can help us learn.

Sometimes the world feels like a big, noisy place. You might feel quite small. Everyone else is busy, or talking, or playing or learning, and you feel as if you are alone.

We all feel lonely sometimes. It's okay.
You will find a friend. It might be someone
who feels just like you do.

Meeting new people often makes us feel shy.

But when we make new friends, we stop feeling shy. Good friends make us feel happy, confident and strong.

With my friends I can be myself!

My friends make me feel giggly!

Anger is a big feeling. It's a scary feeling.

When something upsets us, or annoys us, or frustrates us, it can feel like there is a firework inside that wants to explode.

Sometimes we shout.
We might run off or hit out.
Anger can feel hard to control.

Later, when things are calmer,
we may feel sorry.

**Let's look at
these sums
together.**

Sometimes people show their feelings in unexpected ways. Feelings can be confusing!

I laugh when I feel nervous.

I shout when I'm excited.

And sometimes it is difficult to know how someone else is feeling.

Love isn't a complicated feeling.
It's simple.

Love makes us feel happy and safe.
It makes us feel good about ourselves.

Love can be loud, or quiet. It can feel like a warm hug, a deep laugh, a soft, singing breeze.

Feeling loved helps us love back.

When we talk about our feelings, we help others understand what's really going on inside.

I loved being the winner.

We start to understand ourselves. We start to understand each other, too.

Feelings are important.

Every feeling is normal.

Your feelings help to make you who you are.

Feelings make us feel alive!

How do you think these children are feeling?

Notes for teachers, parents and carers

This book aims to encourage children to talk about their feelings, recognise and value a range of emotions in themselves and those around them, and develop empathy for the way other people may be feeling. The text and images are designed as prompts for discussion, either at home with a parent or carer, or in a classroom setting.

Young children can be encouraged to explore, understand and articulate their own and each other's feelings in a variety of ways. For example, parents and carers can ask a child to look at the different feelings shown throughout the book and say if or when they have felt the same. However, the book should be used sensitively in a classroom setting. If a child discloses feelings of sadness or fear associated with their home life, they may need reassurance that they don't have to share this with their peers but that they can talk to their teacher or another trusted adult instead.

Here are some additional activities that support and expand on the scenarios shown in the book.

How do we show our feelings?

Show children a range of different facial expressions cut from magazines or drawn on flashcards. Ask them how they think that person is feeling. How can they tell? Can they make that face themselves? Discuss how sometimes we express our feelings in different ways, for example, by hiding or shouting or being quiet. Why do we sometimes try to hide our feelings?

Changing feelings

Children can be helped to understand that feelings can change quickly, just like the weather. Make a 'feelings barometer' by cutting out a large circle from a plain piece of cardboard and dividing it into six segments, like slices of pie. Draw a picture of a different type of weather in each segment, for example: sunny, rainbow, raining, thunder and lightning, foggy, chilly, or sunshine and showers.

Attach an arrow to the middle with a paper fastener. In the classroom: ask children to match different feelings to different types of weather, and discuss whether there is a general class atmosphere or mood at any point in the day. At home: encourage your child to turn the arrow to indicate how they are feeling throughout the day.

Creative expression

Music is a wonderful way for young children to explore different feelings. Play a piece of instrumental music that has loud and soft sections, slow and fast sections, and ask them to describe how they feel at different moments in the piece. Alternatively, explore feelings using simple percussion instruments or painting with different colours and brush-strokes.

Coping with strong feelings

Strong feelings can be overwhelming for young children. Teachers, parents and carers can support them by providing a safe way to acknowledge how they feel. Use marker pens on uninflated balloons of different colours to draw faces that are excited, angry and nervous, for example. Then fill the balloons with rice grains, using a funnel, and tie a knot in the opening. Explain that these are the child's balloon buddies. When they have a strong feeling, they can select the balloon that matches how they feel and squeeze it for as long as they need to.

Responding to others

Encourage children to think about how they might respond to each other's feelings, for example: being kind when someone is sad, or sitting next to someone who looks lonely, or telling a teacher if someone is hurt or upset.

Useful words

curious   how it feels when you want to find out about something.

embarrassed   how it feels when people are looking at you and you don't want them to.

frustrated   how it feels when you want to do something but you can't.

impatient   how it feels when you want something or someone to hurry up!

proud   how it feels when you have achieved something new.

Index